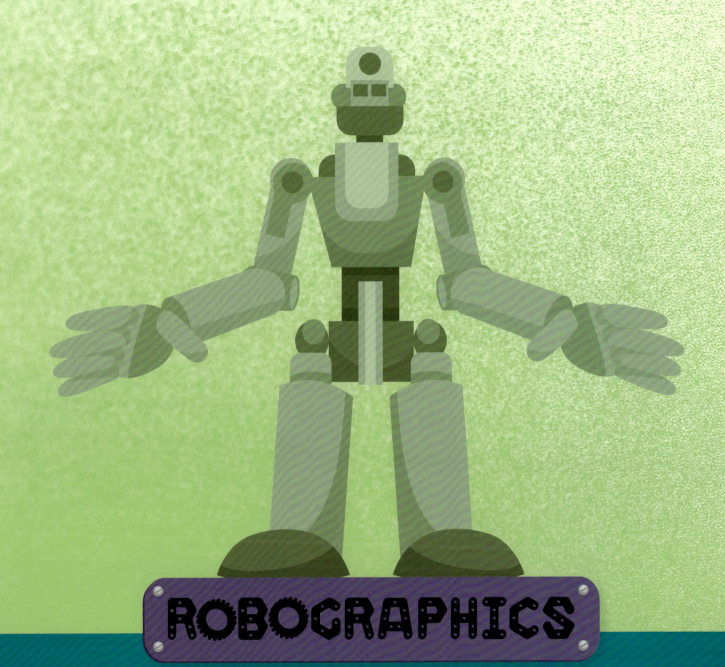

ROBOGRAPHICS

ROBOT EXPLORERS

CLIVE GIFFORD

First published in Great Britain in 2022 by Wayland
© Hodder and Stoughton, 2022

Artwork: Collaborate Agency
Design: Collaborate Agency
Editor: Nicola Edwards

ISBN 978 1 5263 1636 3 (hb) 978 1 5263 1640 0 (pb)

Printed and bound in China

FSC
www.fsc.org
MIX
Paper from responsible sources
FSC® C104740

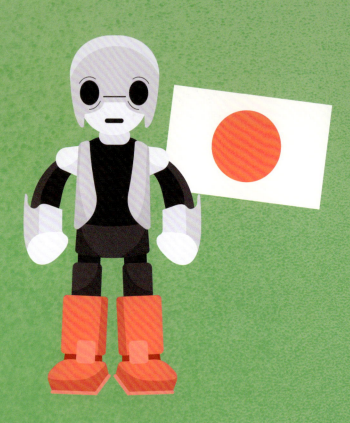

Picture credits:

The publisher would like to thank the following for permission to reproduce their pictures:

Airbus.com: 8

German Research Center for Artificial Intelligence: 4, 18

ETH Zürich Robotic Systems Lab: 11

NASA: 13 (b);19; 20 (t); 24; 29

NASA/Shutterstock: Artsiom P 13 (t)

Wikimedia Commons: 20 (b); 27

Every attempt has been made to clear copyright. Should there be any inadvertent omission please apply to the publisher for rectification.

The website addresses (URLs) included in this book were valid at the time of going to press. However, it is possible that the contents of addresses may have changed since the publication of this book. No responsibility for any such changes can be accepted by either the author or the Publisher.

Wayland, an imprint of
Hachette Children's Group
Part of Hodder and Stoughton
Carmelite House
50 Victoria Embankment
London EC4Y 0DZ

An Hachette UK Company
www.hachette.co.uk
www.hachettechildrens.co.uk

CONTENTS

ROBOT EXPLORERS

Exploration is a risky business. Advances in technology now mean that in many situations we can send machines to explore, rather than risk human lives. Robots are an exciting and particularly versatile type of machine that can be programmed to perform a wide range of tasks. The first mobile robots could only travel short distances, but modern robots venture far and wide, exploring the wildest places imaginable.

Runtime:
3 hours

Weight:
16 kg

Wheel diameter:
41.6 cm

The German robot rover **Asguard IV** (left) can carry a third of its own weight in sensors and scientific instruments. It explores places such as this lava tube in the Canary Islands.

SPACE EXPLORERS

Robots are especially useful in space as they are often far smaller and lighter than spacecraft carrying astronauts. They can also travel on much longer missions than humans, imaging and measuring parts of the solar system for years at a time. The farthest human-made device from Earth is a robotic space probe, Voyager 1. It launched in 1977 and is still going.

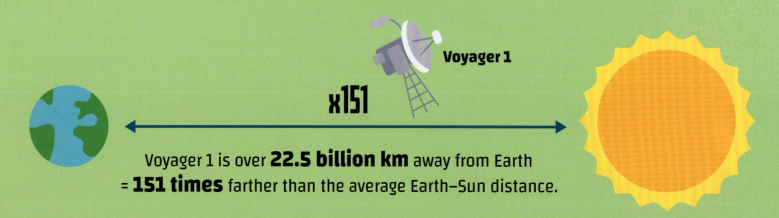

Voyager 1

x151

Voyager 1 is over **22.5 billion km** away from Earth
= **151 times** farther than the average Earth–Sun distance.

HELICOPTERS ON MARS

In February 2021, NASA's Ingenuity became the first robot helicopter to land on Mars. Travelling on board the Perseverance rover (see page 24), Ingenuity was designed to perform test flights of up to 300 m in the Martian air.

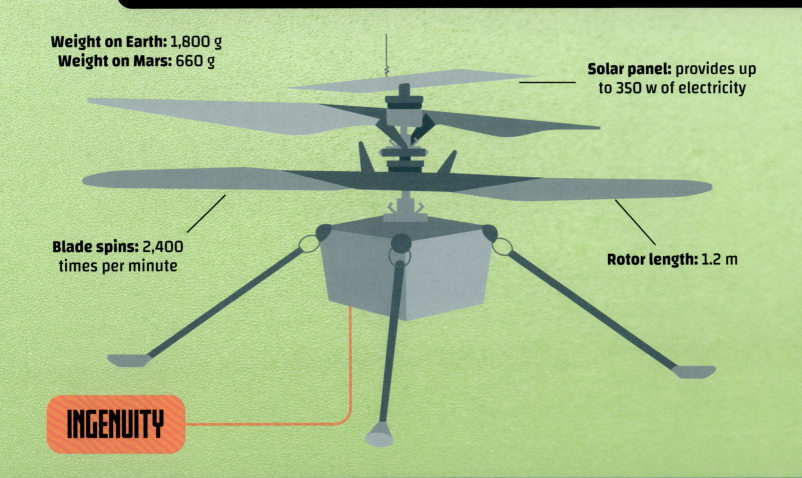

Weight on Earth: 1,800 g
Weight on Mars: 660 g

Solar panel: provides up to 350 w of electricity

Blade spins: 2,400 times per minute

Rotor length: 1.2 m

INGENUITY

GOING UNDERGROUND

Robots are exploring caves and other underground features of our planet. In 2019, for example, the Sunfish autonomous robot mapped the world's largest underground lake in Dragon's Breath Cave, Namibia. It reached depths of 100 m.

Sunfish measures 167 cm x 47 cm x 20 cm – about the size of a cello.

100 m

STRANGE PLACES

While some robots are exploring space, others can be found investigating some surprising locations on Earth. Robots can be built to travel into places that are too small, difficult or deadly for people to explore, or sent on one-way missions with no hope of return.

SHARK-CANO!

One of the first robotic explorers clambered into an active volcano in 1994. Dante II used its eight legs to climb down the inside slopes of a volcanic crater in Mount Spurr, in the US state of Alaska. In 2015, simple, disposable robots from Queensland, Australia, were sent into Kavachi – an undersea Pacific volcano – and found sharks swimming inside!

Dante II weight: 800 kg – more than an F1 car

Crater depth: 200 m

Cable length x diameter:
300 m x 1.1 cm

Descent speed:
approximately 1 cm per second

Power: 2,000 w

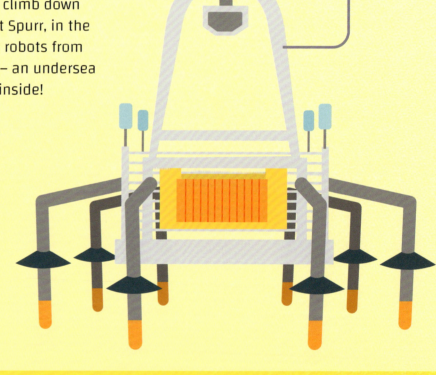

DANTE II

TEMPLES AND PYRAMIDS

Small, narrow robots have been sent down previously unexplored chambers and shafts in ancient temples and Egyptian pyramids. In 2018, several wheeled rovers and an inflating soft robot called Vinebot discovered new passageways littered with human bones deep inside the 3,000-year-old Chavín de Huántar temple in Peru.

FUEL FINDER

Mini Manbo explored part of the damaged Fukushima nuclear power plant in 2017. The remote-controlled underwater robot carried cameras and radiation-measuring sensors. It successfully found the plant's uranium fuel, which had been missing for six years.

Diameter: 13 cm
Length: 30 cm

Lights: 6 x 10 w

Propulsion: five propeller fans

MINI MANBO

Upuaut 2 was the first robot to explore inside the Great Pyramid of Giza in Egypt. The robot's rubber tracks could grip and push along the ceiling as well as the floor.

Electric motors can pull 6.5 times the robot's weight.

UPUAUT 2

Micro video camera can pan left to right and tilt up and down.

Aluminium construction

Height: 28 cm down to 12 cm

Width: 12 cm

Length: 37 cm

Weight: 6 kg

VINEBOT

100 ...

... the number of times its original length, a Vinebot can extend.

AIRBORNE EXPLORATION

Aerial robots vary in size from micro vehicles, which fit in the palm of your hand, to long-distance drones the size of regular aircraft. Without human pilots, these craft can be built lighter, use less fuel and stay in the air longer. They can perform many tasks, from measuring the atmosphere to conducting search-and-rescue missions.

HIGH FLIER

Some long-distance flying robots rely on solar panels on their wings to provide power. Airbus's Zephyr robot (above) uses solar power to recharge its battery packs so that it can fly by day and night. In 2018, it set a robotic world record, with a flight lasting **25 days**, **23 hours** and **57 minutes**.

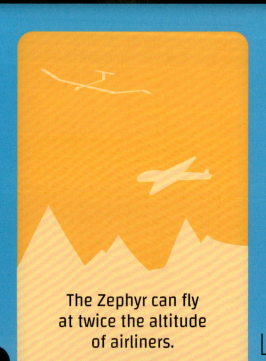

The Zephyr can fly at twice the altitude of airliners.

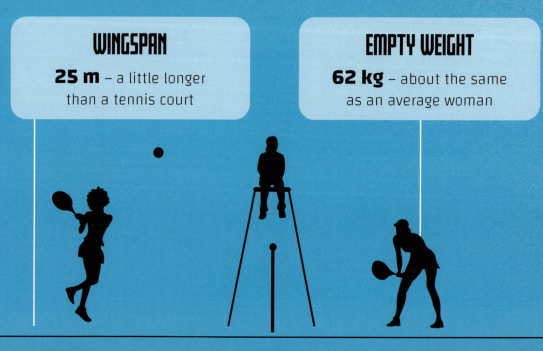

WINGSPAN
25 m – a little longer than a tennis court

EMPTY WEIGHT
62 kg – about the same as an average woman

EYES IN THE SKY

Flying robot drones are used frequently to explore hard-to-reach places. In 2019–2020, drones discovered:

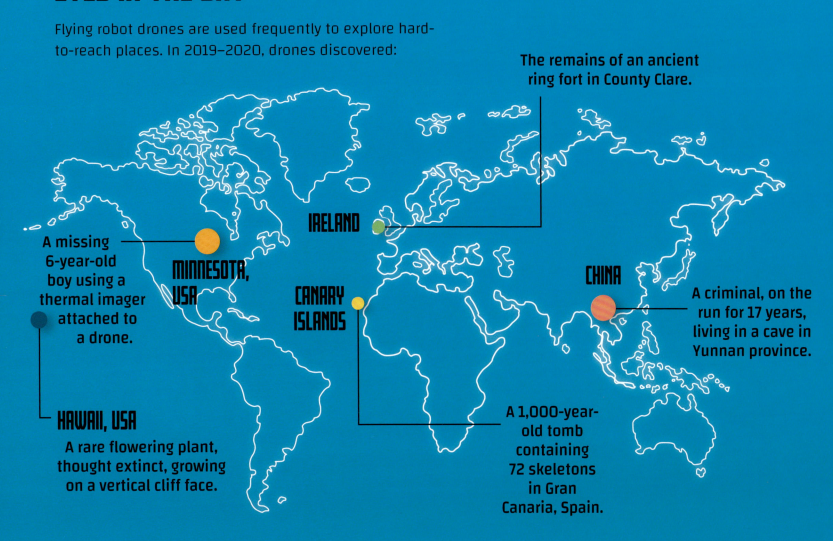

The remains of an ancient ring fort in County Clare.

A missing 6-year-old boy using a thermal imager attached to a drone.

MINNESOTA, USA

IRELAND

CHINA

A criminal, on the run for 17 years, living in a cave in Yunnan province.

CANARY ISLANDS

HAWAII, USA

A rare flowering plant, thought extinct, growing on a vertical cliff face.

A 1,000-year-old tomb containing 72 skeletons in Gran Canaria, Spain.

IN A FLAP

Some smaller robots copy the wing movements of insects, such as bees and dragonflies, to create lift. Future versions may be able to navigate themselves outdoors and perform useful tasks from the air.

	BionicOpter	eMotion Butterfly	RoboBee
Weight:	175 g	32 g	0.08 g
Wingspan:	63 cm	50 cm	3 cm
Flaps per second:	15–20	1–3	120

ROBO-PROBES

Some robots are out of this world! Space probes are machines with robotic features that leave Earth and its gravity to orbit round or land on and explore other planets, moons, asteroids or comets in our solar system. Some make astonishingly long journeys.

MARS RECONNAISSANCE ORBITER (MRO)

Arriving at Mars in 2006 and still working today, the MRO navigates itself as it orbits the planet exploring its atmosphere and taking images. By 2020, the probe had sent back 379 terabits of data – more than all other missions to planets put together.

Speed:
3.4 km per second

Total orbits:
over 60,000

Time per orbit:
112 minutes

Images taken:
378,000 – enough to fill **1,575** 240-picture photo albums

NASA's New Horizons probe took less than 10 years to travel 4.82 billion km to reach the dwarf planet Pluto. In a 900 km/h jet airliner, that journey would take 611 years.

SPEEDIEST IN SPACE

In 2020, the Parker Solar Probe reached 393,044 km/h making it the fastest ever machine.

That's:

802 x
faster than the world's fastest sports car

422 x
faster than a typical jet airliner

As it gets closer to the Sun, the Parker Solar Probe is expected to break its own record, reaching up to 690,000 km/h. At that speed, a round-the-world trip would take under **4 seconds**.

JUPITER EXPLORER

Juno spent five years travelling to Jupiter before going into orbit around the solar system's largest planet. The probe spins about itself once every 30 seconds so all nine of its scientific instruments get to measure parts of the planet.

3 x 20 m² solar panels are needed to power the craft as sunlight is 25 x weaker at Jupiter than Earth.

3.5 m x 3.5 m box houses scientific instruments

Jupiter is so large that you could fit **1,300** planet Earths inside it.

SAMPLES FROM SPACE

Most robots and probes are sent on one-way missions into space. Japan's Hayabusa2 probe (left) returned to Earth in December 2020 carrying samples of a distant asteroid called Ryugu. The six-year mission also dropped three small rover robots on to the asteroid's surface to explore it.

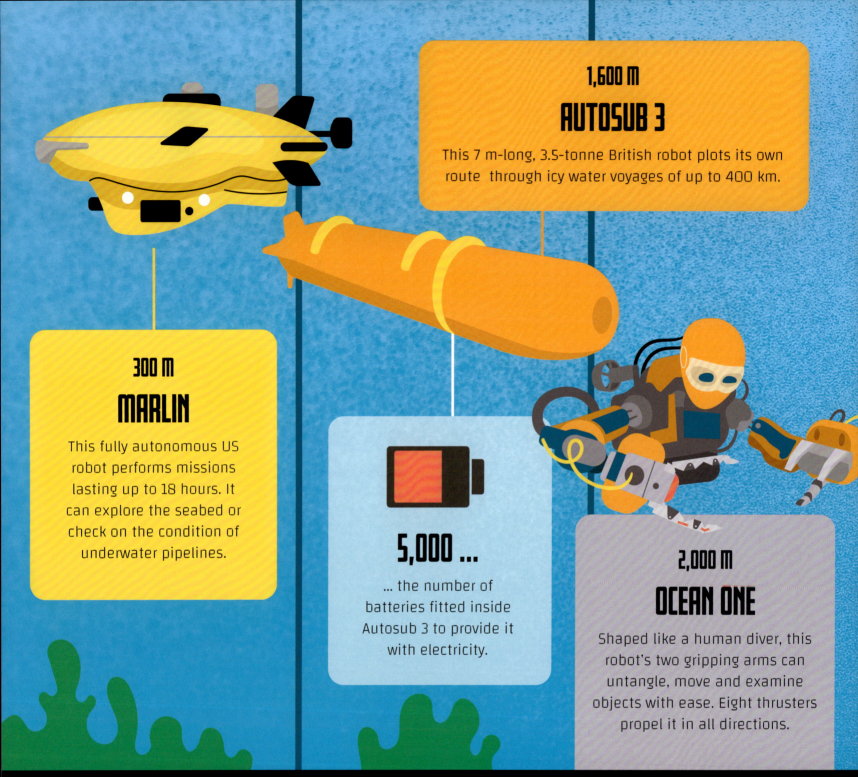

1,600 M

AUTOSUB 3

This 7 m-long, 3.5-tonne British robot plots its own route through icy water voyages of up to 400 km.

300 M

MARLIN

This fully autonomous US robot performs missions lasting up to 18 hours. It can explore the seabed or check on the condition of underwater pipelines.

5,000 ...

... the number of batteries fitted inside Autosub 3 to provide it with electricity.

2,000 M

OCEAN ONE

Shaped like a human diver, this robot's two gripping arms can untangle, move and examine objects with ease. Eight thrusters propel it in all directions.

DEEPWATER EXPLORERS

With an average depth of 3,600 km, much of the world's oceans remain a mystery – out of people's range to explore easily. Underwater robots, however, can investigate large areas without the need for oxygen and life-saving systems. Water pressure mounts quickly the deeper you dive. At 1,000 m or more, it would crush a car with ease. So, deep-diving robots are built to be incredibly strong.

In 2015, REMUS 6000 discovered a Spanish galleon shipwreck, the San José, which sank in the Atlantic in 1708. Aboard is believed to be **US $17 billion** worth of gold and silver!

11,000 m
KAIKO

About the size of a small car, this Japanese robot recovered a sunken space rocket and in 1995 was the first robot to dive to the deepest point on Earth, Challenger Deep in the Pacific Ocean.

6,000 m
REMUS 6000

Electric motors spinning a two-bladed propeller allow this 3.96 m-long robot to travel at 8.2 km/h. Its missions last up to 22 hours.

4,500 m
SUBASTIAN

This 3.2-tonne robot uses its five thrusters to move through deep waters searching for exciting new signs of life. The robot has 24 lights to illuminate the gloomy ocean depths and films with four HD cameras.

The maximum depth Kaikō reached equalled **33 Eiffel Towers** stacked on top of each other.

 x 33

WALKING AND ROLLING

Legged robots can walk, climb, cross gaps and step over obstacles, often with less risk of getting stuck than wheeled robots. This agility takes a lot of processing power – precise positions of all body parts have to be calculated and their movements coordinated. Thousands of calculations may have to be made each second to allow a robot to move and keep its balance.

19 ...

... the number of times in a row a one-legged robot, built by Disney Research, could hop before losing its balance.

340,000 ...

... the number of steps taken by the Xingzhe No. 1 four-legged robot in one trip before it needed to recharge its batteries. The robot covered 134.03 km in 54 hours.

20 ...

... the number of times that the six-legged MAX robot is lighter than similar-sized robots. Built by CSIRO in Australia, the **M**ulti-legged **A**utonomous e**X**plorer stands 2.25 m tall and weighs 60 kg.

MOCHIBOT

The Mochibot (right) from Japan boasts an astonishing 32 legs! Each leg is made of three parts that telescope together. Electric actuators can retract or extend each leg. Mochibot can move smoothly in any direction simply by pulling in or pushing out different legs to change its overall shape.

Mochibot's maximum size of 1 m across is double its minimum size, with all its legs pulled in.

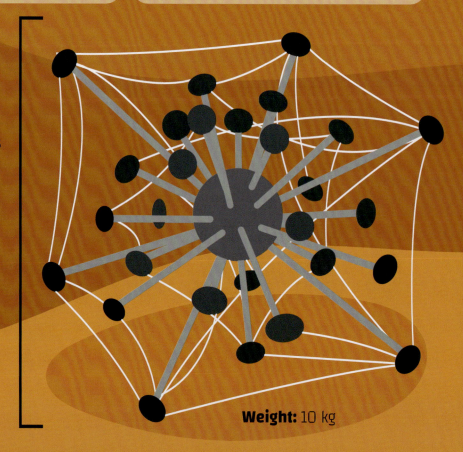

Weight: 10 kg

TUMBLEWEED ROVER

Why walk on legs when you can roll? Some future explorers may be spherical, allowing them to roll across uneven ground using as little power as possible. Team Tumbleweed's ball-shaped rover (below) folds flat like a pop-up tent, so the 100 rovers planned for 2026 could be carried on a single spacecraft. When unfurled, the giant ball, made of super-strong titanium, would use its sails to be blown around Mars, exploring more quickly than legged rover designs.

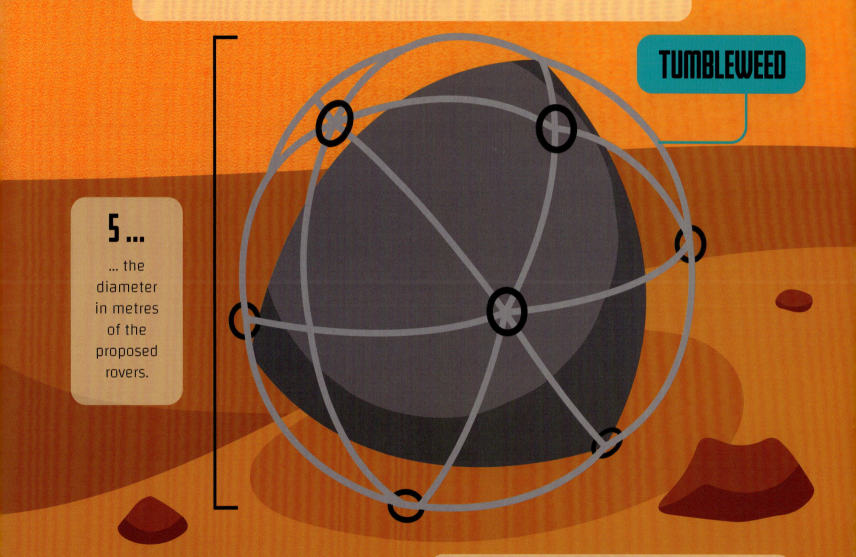

100 M² ...

... the area of the robot's sails – about the size of 24 table tennis tables.

TUMBLEWEED

5 ...

... the diameter in metres of the proposed rovers.

360 ...

... the maximum speed in km/h of winds on Mars.

30 GB ...

... the amount of science data 100 Tumbleweed rovers rolling around the surface of Mars would generate *every second*.

DESERT EXPLORERS

Deserts, hot and cold, provide some of the toughest tests for robot explorers, often a long way away from human support. They may be battered by high winds and encounter treacherous conditions beneath their wheels, tracks or legs. Their electronics can struggle with extreme temperatures. It takes really robust robots to deal with all these challenges.

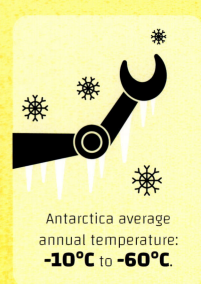

Antarctica average annual temperature: **-10°C** to **-60°C**.

SHERPA TT

This German wheeled rover navigated itself over 1,300 m of tough, steeply sloping Moroccan desert in 2018–19 tests. Its unusual design means that the legs can rise inwards and the body upwards so the robot can clear obstacles or the legs can spread out for maximum stability.

Sherpa TT footprint:
1 m x 1 m to 2.4 m x 2.4 m

Height:
0.8 m to 1.8 m

Main battery:
8,000–10,000 mAh (milliAmp hour)– just twice the capacity of a large smartphone battery

Run time:
1.5 hours

HOT AND COLD

The NOMAD robot rover (right) has navigated successfully around Chile's hot Atacama Desert and Antarctica's icy coastal land.

NOMAD'S ACHIEVEMENTS

7 meteorites
discovered in Antarctica

Explored
2,500 m²
of icefields

45-day, 215 km-long trek
through Atacama Desert

POP-UP BOT

Earth's deserts make ideal testing grounds for robot designs that may one day explore other planets or moons. NASA's A-PUFFER (Pop-Up Flat Folding Explorer Robot) folds up to take up little space or to fit between gaps in rocks. It unfolds to roll along on its powered wheels.

Distance from human controllers:
at least 7,200 km

Weight:
720 kg

Top speed:
1.8 km/h

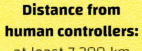

NOMAD

ANDROID ASTRONAUTS

Sending a human astronaut into space also means sending lots of supplies and life support technology with them. Humanoid robots can provide an extra pair of hands and eyes without the need for additional food, water and oxygen. Future humanoid robots may perform riskier tasks, such as spacewalks outside of a spacecraft, to carry out repairs or assemble space bases.

ROBONAUT R2

Arriving at the International Space Station (ISS) in 2011, Robonaut R2 spent over seven years in space – far more than any other humanoid robot. Its brains are in its stomach and its head is crammed with five cameras. The robot gained a pair of legs in space in 2014 and proved capable of performing simple tasks and experiments, including catching floating tools.

Height (without legs): 101.6 cm

Legs: 2.7 m long

Weight: 149.7 kg

350 ...

... the number of sensors fitted inside Robonaut R2, along with 38 computer processors.

2.2KG ...

... the maximum amount of gripping force applied by each of Robonaut R2's four fingers.

VALKYRIE

This NASA robot remains on Earth while engineers and researchers test out ways in which robots could aid astronauts in space. Seven joints in each arm and 38 sensors in each four-fingered hand give the robot the dexterity to handle and operate power tools.

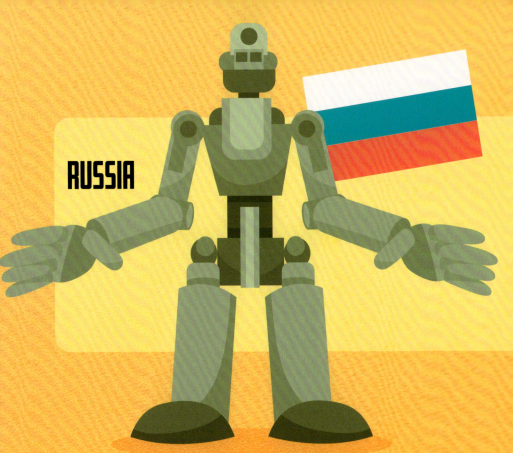

RUSSIA

FEDOR

Soyuz, ISS, 2019

1.8 m tall

Tested new emergency rescue system on the Soyuz spacecraft and used tools, such as drills, in space.

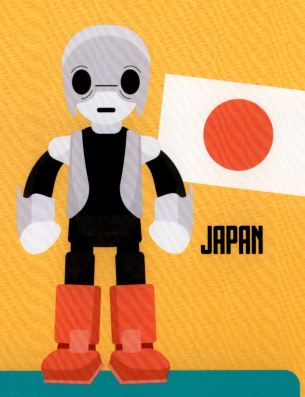

JAPAN

INDIA

KIROBO

ISS, 2013–2015

34 cm tall

Robot companion and the first to hold a conversation in space. Could recognise and talk with human astronauts.

VYOMMITRA

Gaganyaan, 2020, 2021

80 cm tall

Tested out spacecraft controls on two unmanned space missions in advance of India's planned first human spaceflight.

FINDING THE WAY

Some robots are remotely controlled by a human operator. Others have to find their own way and rely on their programming and sensors. These mostly bounce light or sound off objects to measure distances and spot obstacles and hazards. With this and other information, the robot can identify what lies ahead and plan its best route.

Wheel encoders: measure how far the wheel turns to compute how far the robot has travelled.

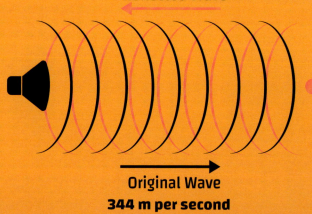

Reflected Wave

344 M ...

... the typical distance sound travels per second through air (when temperature = 20°C).

Original Wave
344 m per second

Cliff sensors: bounce sound or light off the ground to detect holes or ledges. They can alert a robot to change direction to avoid a dangerously steep drop.

Ultrasound sensors: emit high-pitched sound pulses and calculate the time it takes them to bounce back from objects to gauge distances.

IR sensors: emit beams of infrared light, which reflect off objects to measure distances.

Contact sensors: consist of a switch or wire filament that registers a signal if they touch something.

MAKING LIGHT WORK

Light Detection And Ranging (LiDAR) sends out repeated pulses of light and converts the time they take to bounce back into distances. A ground LiDAR fitted to a mobile robot can rotate to build up a 360° map in three dimensions of a robot's surroundings. The robot's controller and other sensors can identify targets and obstacles from the map and plot a safe route through.

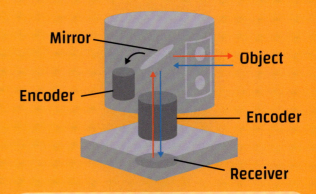

Mirror

Object

Encoder

Encoder

Receiver

500,000 ...

... the number of pulses of light some LiDAR systems fire per second.

FLYING LIDAR

Some UAVs (Unmanned Aerial Vehicles) have been equipped with LiDAR to survey and explore the land below. They can produce precise maps of isolated areas and even spot ancient sites or structures below forests, such as a previously unknown Maya city found in Guatemala in 2018.

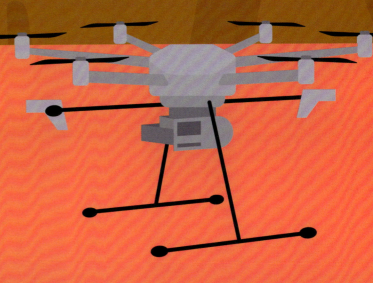

ROVING ROUND MARS

Four generations of NASA robot rovers have explored Mars, starting with Sojourner in 1997. These robots have to withstand extreme temperatures and be reliable – engineers cannot nip over from Earth to Mars to make repairs! Radio signals take minutes to travel between the planets, so robot rovers need to be smart enough to make on-the-spot decisions themselves.

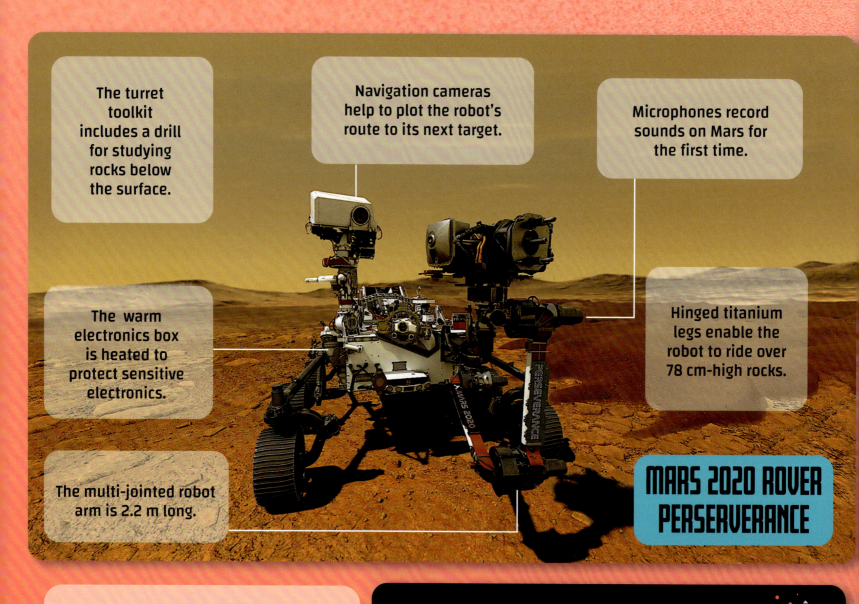

The turret toolkit includes a drill for studying rocks below the surface.

Navigation cameras help to plot the robot's route to its next target.

Microphones record sounds on Mars for the first time.

The warm electronics box is heated to protect sensitive electronics.

Hinged titanium legs enable the robot to ride over 78 cm-high rocks.

The multi-jointed robot arm is 2.2 m long.

MARS 2020 ROVER PERSERVERANCE

TEMPERATURE RANGE ON MARS

+30°C

-140°C

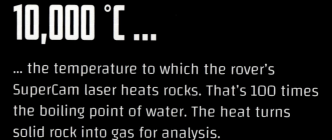

10,000 °C ...

... the temperature to which the rover's SuperCam laser heats rocks. That's 100 times the boiling point of water. The heat turns solid rock into gas for analysis.

GOING THE DISTANCE

Mars rovers work for months or years, but at low speed. Perseverance's top speed of 4.2 cm per second (152 m per hour) might sound sluggish, but is actually 10.5 times faster than Sojourner. Mars rovers are getting heavier, too. The latest weighs as much as a small car.

PERSEVERANCE

Arrival: February 2021

Dimensions: 3 m x 2.7 m x 2.2 m

Weight: 1,025 kg

Cameras: 23

Power: Power: 110 w (plutonium and batteries)

SOJOURNER

Arrival: July 1997

Dimensions: 63 cm x 48 cm x 30 cm

Weight: 10.5 kg

Cameras: 3

Power: 15 w (solar panels and battery)

MARS EXPLORATION ROVER (MER)-A & MER-B

Arrival: January 2004

Dimensions: 1.6 m x 2.3 m

Weight: 185kg

Cameras: 9

Power: 140w (solar panels and battery)

CURIOSITY

Arrival: August 2012

Dimensions: 3 m x 2.7 m x 2.2 m

Weight: 899 kg

Cameras: 17

Power: 110 w (plutonium and batteries)

ROBOT SWARMS

Most robot explorers work alone, but that could all change in the future. Research into large groups of small, simple robots, known as swarms, could lead to amazing exploration possibilities. Swarms could share sensing to explore as a whole, but send off smaller numbers to investigate a particular feature. On risky explorations, losing one swarm robot wouldn't be a disaster as others could replace it.

BIONICANTS

Swarm robots may mimic how real ants and other insects work together. These six-legged robots share information with one another over a wireless computer network in order to cooperate and perform a task.

A BionicANT weighs 105g, takes 10mm-long steps and can run for 40 minutes on a battery with a tenth of the capacity of a smartphone.

UNDERWATER SWARMS

Aquabotix SwarmDivers from Australia communicate with each other using radio waves. They could be used in groups to patrol ports or in larger numbers to measure water quality or to map areas of the seabed.

Dimensions: 75 cm x 13 cm x 45 cm

SWARMDIVER

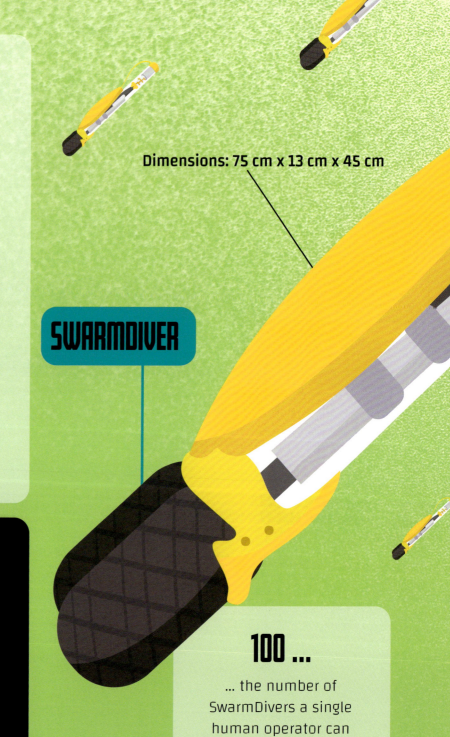

100 ...

... the number of SwarmDivers a single human operator can control at the same time.

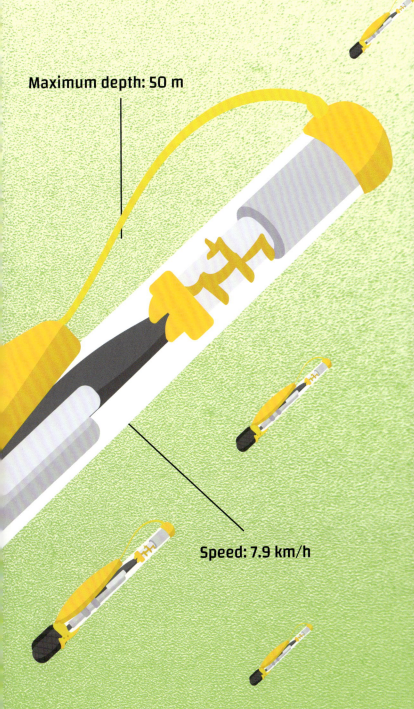

Maximum depth: 50 m

Speed: 7.9 km/h

WORKING TOGETHER

Kilobots are a group of 1,024 identical robots built to investigate how future robot swarms could work. The tiny, 33 mm-diameter Kilobots communicate with each other using infrared signals and can form shapes or follow a lead robot.

33 mm

Working together, over 1,000 Kilobots move to form a star-shape.

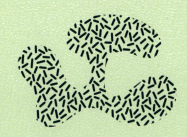

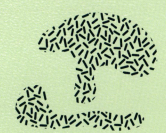

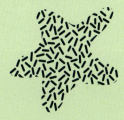

Robots travel
1 cm per second

7 cm
cmmunication range with other Kilobots

Run time of
2.5 hours
between recharges

FUTURE EXPLORERS

From swarms of tiny ground-exploring bots to mighty robot astronauts, the future of robotic exploration is exciting. Advances in materials, computing and technologies such as 3D printing, are helping to create an amazing range of designs. New robots will investigate hard-to-reach places on land and deep underwater in increasingly innovative ways.

95% ...

... the percentage of the ocean floor that has not yet been fully explored and mapped.

BUILD-A-BOT

Future soft robots, made of strong, flexible materials, might be able to add or remove different body parts for a range of exploration tasks.

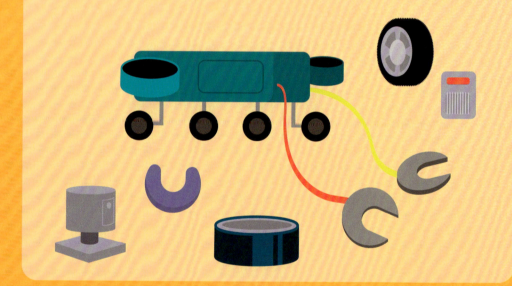

ENERGY FROM OCEANS

Future ocean robots may harness power from the waters they explore to cruise on endless voyages. Saltwater batteries, harnessing wave energy and fuel cells that turn fish waste into electricity are all being investigated.

11,400 ...

... the number of terawatt-hours of electricity potentially found in ocean waves – equal to the electricity produced by 300–400 nuclear power plants.

SHAPE-SHIFTING BOTS

Future robots on land and underwater may be able to change shape to swim, fly or crawl depending on what they need to explore. NASA's Shapeshifter robots may one day explore other moons and planets. The robots' parts would fit together to form a rolling ball but could detach to act as separate flying or swimming robots.

IN THE AIR

Flying robots could explore far greater areas than robotic rovers on the ground. NASA plans to send a hefty quadcopter robot, called Dragonfly, to explore Titan, Saturn's largest moon, in 2026. Titan has a thick atmosphere and 1/7th the gravity of Earth, which would make it easier for a heavy robot to fly and explore.

DRAGONFLY

Power:
8 x 1 m rotor blades

Speed:
about 36 km/h

Altitude:
up to 4,000 m

Range:
8–10 km per flight

DRAGONFLY'S TASKS

Analyse the chemicals in soil and rocks

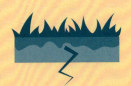

Measure earthquakes and other seismic activity underground

Photograph key moon features

Study weather and atmosphere on Titan

Identify suitable landing sites for future missions

QUIZ

Try this quiz to find out how much you can remember about robot explorers. The answers are at the bottom of the page.

1. How many legs does the Mochibot robot have?
   a) 4
   b) 8
   c) 32

2. Which robot made a 25-day flight without landing?
   a) Kaiko
   b) Zephyr
   c) RoboBee

3. Which humanoid robot was the first to hold a conversation in space?
   a) Kirobo
   b) Robonaut R2
   c) Fedor

4. How many times do the blades on the Ingenuity robot helicopter spin per minute?
   a) 600
   b) 1,200
   c) 2,400

5. How many batteries are fitted inside Autosub 3?
   a) 8
   b) 24
   c) 5,000

6. Which robot explored icefields, hot deserts and found seven meteorites in Antarctica?
   a) Dragonfly
   b) NOMAD
   c) Sojourner

7. What is the farthest machine away from Earth?
   a) Voyager 1
   b) Mars Rover 2020 (Perseverance)
   c) BionicANTs

8. How many cameras does the Perseverance rover carry?
   a) 8
   b) 14
   c) 23

9. What is the maximum depth at which a SwarmDiver robot can operate?
   a) 50 m
   b) 200 m
   c) 3,000 m

10. In which US state did the Dante II robot climb down a live volcano?
    a) Washington
    b) Alaska
    c) California

Answers
1.c, 2.b, 3.a, 4.c, 5.c, 6.b, 7.a, 8.c, 9.a, 10.b

30

GLOSSARY

actuator
A device like an electric motor that moves another part.

altitude
The height of an object above sea level.

atmosphere
The blanket of gases that surrounds a planet.

autonomous
Describes a machine that makes decisions and works by itself.

controller
The part of the robot that makes decisions and tells the other parts of the robot what to do. It is usually a computer.

dexterity
The ability to handle and manipulate objects with grippers, tools or hands.

disposable
Describes something that is not used permanently, but can be discarded after use.

drone
A pilot-less flying machine, usually flown by a person on the ground using a remote control.

humanoid
Describes a robot that has a partial or complete human-like appearance or one that performs human-like actions.

hydraulics
A power system using liquids in cylinders that is found in some robots.

infrared
A type of electromagnetic radiation, like light, but not visible to our eyes.

sensor
A device that collects information about a robot or its surroundings.

spherical
Describes something that is round like a ball in all three dimensions.

terabit
A measure of computer data or memory equal to one trillion bits (binary digits).

thermal imager
A device that detects infrared radiation given off by warm things.

FURTHER INFORMATION

BOOKS

A Robot World, Clive Gifford, Franklin Watts, 2019

Adventures in STEAM: Robots, Izzi Howell, Wayland, 2019

WEBSITES

https://spectrum.ieee.org/aerospace/robotic-exploration
Keep up to date with the latest news on robotic exploration research and journeys.

https://mars.nasa.gov/mars2020/
The official website of the Mars 2020 mission, including the rover Perseverance and the robot helicopter Ingenuity.

www.youtube.com/watch?v=loHzoeFP9Io
Watch the RoboBee mini robot take to the air.

INDEX